22 SOAP MAKING RECIPES IN UNDER 20 MINUTES

NATURAL BEAUTIFUL SOAPS FROM HOME
WITH COLORING AND FRAGRANCE

DAPHNE BIRD

CONTENTS

Getting Started With Soap Making — v

1. Option 1 — 1
2. Option 2 — 3
3. Option 3 — 5
4. Hand and Body Soap — 7
5. Foaming Hand Soap — 9
6. Foaming Face Cleanse — 10
7. Bar Face Soap — 12
8. Lathering Skin Bar — 14
9. Liquid Body Soaps — 16
10. Soap Paint — 18
11. Holiday Soaps — 20
12. New Year's Eve Soap — 21
13. Birthday Cake Soap with Frosting — 23
14. American Flag - Presidents Day Bar Soap — 27
15. Valentine's Day Soap — 30
16. National Women's Day — 32
17. Lucky Shamrock Soaps — 33
18. Easter Egg Soaps — 35
19. Earth Day Soaps — 37
20. Cinco De Mayo Soaps — 39
21. Mother's Day Soap — 42
22. Father's Day Coffee Soap — 44
23. Spooky Halloween Soap — 46
24. Thanksgiving Soap Recipe — 48
25. Christmas Soap — 50
26. I hope you enjoyed My Creations — 53

22 Soap Making Recipes in Under 20 Minutes by Daphne Bird Published by BadgerS Publishing

© 2020 Daphne Bird

All rights reserved. No portion of this book may be reproduced in any form without permission from the publisher, except as permitted by U.S. copyright law. For permissions contact:

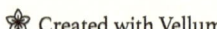 Created with Vellum

GETTING STARTED WITH SOAP MAKING

Whether you're looking for a D.I.Y. for a homemade spa, looking for a fun little project, or you're looking to start your own little self-care business, there are a few things you will need to know. Before you start your project, you need to have an action plan!

You need to take into consideration all the different types of soaps you can make. You should also plan out what fragrances are compatible with skin and make sure, if you would like to add color, to check and see if those pigments will stain or not.

It is all up to you on how you want the type or texture of the soap to be. Would you like bar soap? Perhaps a gel or foam? Are you going to add exfoliants? There are so many questions to be answered! Well I'm here to make decision making easy and to do all your research for you.

In the next pages, you'll find the 3 optional additions to add to any soap making recipe. Choose whether or not you are going to include color, fragrance and lye in your homemade soap.

1

OPTION 1
COLOR

If you decide to add color into your fancy homemade soap recipe, there are some very important, key things you need to take into consideration. When purchasing a dye, or even using a product you already have at home, it's vital to check and see if it's going to stain your skin or other surfaces. I don't know about you, but I personally don't feel like having dark purple skin for a few weeks!

If you're looking to dye your soaps naturally, here are some suggestions for you:

- **Alfalfa:** using dried, ground alfalfa will give your soap a medium green coloring.
- **Carrots:** Use ground up raw carrots to give your soap a yellow-orange color.
- **Chamomile:** To produce a beige to yellowish color, you can use dried, powdered chamomile.
- **Cocoa Powder:** Brown color.
- **Coffee:** Using finely ground coffee is sure to give you a dark brown to black colored soap. As a plus it will also act as an exfoliant and it can remove odors.
- **Paprika:** Orange color
- **Poppy Seeds:** Not exactly a color, but it will give it black specks and also act as an exfoliant.
- **Rose Pink Clay:** Not only does it draw out impurities in your skin, but it gives off a brownish pink color.
- **Spearmint:** Use dried, ground up spearmint to receive a green or brown color.
- **Spinach:** Produces a light green color when dried and ground up.

IF YOU'RE NOT into any of those options, there is always the option of buying coloration or other soap supplies from various online vendors.

2
OPTION 2
FRAGRANCE

Like with the color, you can choose to buy fragrance oils or you can make them yourself! If you're still interested in the natural route, here are some more options for you:

- Almond
- Cinnamon
- Cloves
- French Lavender
- Jasmine
- Orange
- Peppermint
- Rose
- Sage
- Vanilla

Before you start, be sure not to use any equipment you would use for your cooking. Do **not** use copper or aluminum as well as any plastic mixing bowls that might melt. For a mold, use silicone. You may find molds at a local crafts store or even on an online website such as amazon. Some things you will want to keep close by are anything you plan on adding to the soap, a towel, stainless steel thermometer, and a pint canning jar.

You can add aloe vera gel to your soaps along with dry milk powder, oatmeal, ground coffee, cornmeal, and salt are just a few.

3

OPTION 3

LYE

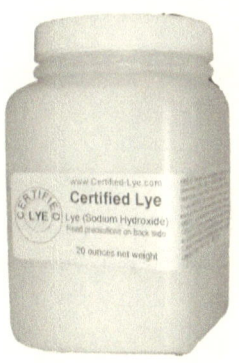

Many people tend to get nervous when I mention lye and they use it as a reason not to get into soap making at all. However, Lye is nothing to worry about when handled properly.

What is Lye?

The chemical process of making soap is referred to as

saponification. It includes an alkali (lye), combined with vegetable oils to cause a chemical reaction. This reaction breaks down the fats or oils into fatty acid chains, and the lye is neutralized in the process.

Lye is something you cannot substitute with when making soaps. Always use lye in crystal form or **100% sodium hydroxide**.

Consider this: Your solution will be just pools of fat and oil, without using lye in your recipe.

CAUTION: I have outlined some important notes on working with lye below:

USE GLOVES AND EYE PROTECTION, even a mask if you desire, when working with lye. Lye can burn holes in fabric or leave burns on your skin. When lye is mixed with water, it will heat up and fume for about thirty seconds to a minute. It may cause a choking sensation, but don't worry, this is not permanent and should pass in a few minutes.

ALWAYS ADD LYE TO WATER, not water to lie. Begin stirring right away and do not allow it to clump along the bottom. That would cause the danger of it heating up all at once and causing an explosion. Although lye might be somewhat dangerous to work with, no lye will remain in your finished soap once it reacts with the oils. Essential oils are very necessary for making soaps along with other oils as stated above.

4

HAND AND BODY SOAP

RECIPE

Ingredients:

- ⅔ cup coconut oil
- ⅔ cup olive oil
- ⅔ cup other liquid oil (such as almond oil or sunflower oil)
- ¼ cup lye
- ¾ cup cool distilled or purified water

Directions:

1. After putting your gloves and protective gear on, cover your workspace with newspapers.
2. Measure your water into the quart jar and have a spoon ready.
3. Make sure you have exactly ¼ cup of lye. Slowly pour the lye into the water and stir as you do so.

Stand back to avoid fumes. When the water clears you can move on to the next step.

4. Add your three oils together in the pint jar. Microwave them for about a minute. The temperature of your oils should be about 120° and your lye should have cooled down to about the same temp.
5. Wait for both to cool to anywhere between 95-105 degrees.
6. Pour the oils into the mixing bowl and slowly add the lye whilst stirring. Stir by hand for five minutes.
7. You can now quit stirring or even use an immersion blender.
8. The mixture will lighten in color and thicken.
9. Once the soap is at "trace" it will look like vanilla pudding and you're good to go.
10. Add your essential oils, herbs, or whatever else you plan to add at this point. Combine thoroughly.
11. Pour the soap into your molds and cover with plastic wrap. Set in an old towel and wrap it up.
12. Check your soap after 24 hours, if it is still soft or warm you should let it sit for another 12-24 hours.
13. Once soap is cooled, turn it over onto a cooling rack or piece of parchment. Allow soap to cure for about four weeks, turning it over once a week to allow it to breathe.

- Keep your soap wrapped up or in an airtight container once the soap is fully cured.

FOAMING HAND SOAP

RECIPE

Ingredients:

- 12 ounces of distilled or boiled water
- 2 Tablespoons of Liquid Castile Soap
- ½ tsp liquid olive or almond oil
- (optional) essential oils

Directions:

1. Fill the dispenser with water one inch from the top
2. Add 2 Tablespoons of liquid castile soap (do NOT add the soap first - pour water before this)
3. Add almond or olive oil plus any essential oils
4. Close and lightly swish

FOAMING FACE CLEANSE

RECIPE

Ingredients:

- ¼ cup of castile soap
- ¼ cup water
- 2 tsp. Of almond or coconut oil
- 2 tsp. Aloe vera gel
- 2 tsp. Glycerin
- 8-12 drops of essential oils (optional)
- Exfoliants (optional)

Directions:

1. Mix all ingredients EXCEPT the soap in a blender.
2. Smell mixture to see if you'd like to add more essential oils.

3. Mix soap into the product slowly.
4. If the soap is still foamy when you pour it into the container, let it sit before adding the cap.

BAR FACE SOAP
RECIPE

Ingredients:

- 6 oz distilled water
- 6 oz aloe vera gel
- 2 oz castor oil
- 4 oz cocoa butter
- 4 oz coconut oil
- 12 oz olive oil
- 5 oz palm oil
- 5 oz palm kernal flakes
- 4.4 oz lye
- 2.5 tablespoon drawing clay
- 1 oz essential oil (I suggest palmrosa, patchouli, rosewood, lemongrass, or lavender or all together)

Directions:

1. In a heat safe bowl mix water and aloe vera, add lye and stir until dissolved.
2. Weigh and melt all oils in a double boiler and stir in the clay. Then remove from heat.
3. Cool both lye mixture and oils to 110-120 degrees.
4. Combine oils and lye slowly, stirring until you get a light trace.
5. Add essential oils and pour into mold.

8

LATHERING SKIN BAR

RECIPE

Ingredients:

- 33 oz coconut oil (76 degree*)
- 4.83 oz lye
- 12.54 oz water
- 0.5-1 ounce essential oils (optional)

Equipment:

- 8-quart crock pot
- Stick blender
- Digital scale
- Thermometer
- Glass measuring cups
- Small glass bowls
- Plastic spoon
- Rubber spatula

- sink/bowl filled with vinegar and water for cleaning up lye
- Protective equipment
- Soap molds
- Parchment paper for lining soap mold

Directions:

1. Weigh your ingredients and set your crockpot on low
2. Slowly add lye to water in a medium sized glass bowl
3. Let lye cool for 5-10 minutes
4. Let coconut oil heat in a saucepan to 120-130F.
5. Pour coconut oil in crockpot and set to low
6. Add lye to crockpot and be careful not to splash and gently stir
7. Use the stick blender and mix to "trace"
8. Cover and cook and low for about 45-60 minutes
9. When checking if the soap is ready it should look like Vaseline and no oil puddles
10. Wait until the mixture cools if you plan to add essential oils
11. Spoon mixture into your mold and let cool
12. Cut soap as soon as it's cool and firm
13. Place bars in a place with good air flow and let them dry for another few days.

LIQUID BODY SOAPS

RECIPE

Ingredients: (1)

- ⅓ cup liquid castile soap
- ¼ cup full fat coconut milk
- 10-15 drops of essential oils

Ingredients: (2)

- ½ cup liquid castile soap
- ½ cup raw honey
- ½ cup coconut oil
- 20 drops of essential oil

Ingredients: (3)

- ½ cup castile oil

- 1 tbsp raw honey
- 2 tsp vegetable glycerin
- 1 tsp vitamin E oil
- 1 tsp olive oil
- 10 drops essential oils

Directions:

1. Pick one set of ingredients and mix thoroughly - pour into a pump or squeeze bottle when done.

10
SOAP PAINT
RECIPE

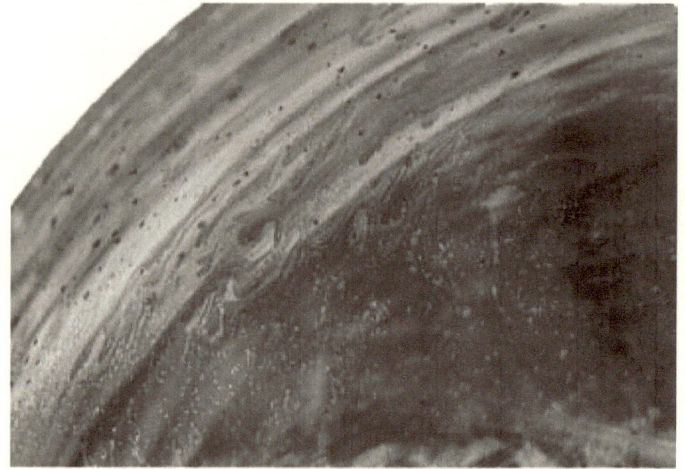

Directions:

1. Mix 2 parts liquid soap, 1-part clear melt, and 1 part rubbing alcohol in a small mixing bowl.

2. Heat in microwave for fifteen seconds and mix well

11

HOLIDAY SOAPS

INTRODUCTION

These recipes are meant to inspire you to create on your own!

Yes, these are great for each holiday, but you can also change the color or fragrance to make it applicable to any day of the year!

Enjoy!

12

NEW YEAR'S EVE SOAP

COLORFUL SOAP RECIPES

Ingredients:

- Clear melt
- White melt
- Champagne fragrance oil
- Basic rectangle mold
- Light gold mica
- Brownie pan
- Numerical cookie cutters
- Rubbing alcohol

Directions:

1. Melt five oz of white soap base in the microwave
2. Pour soap into rubber brownie pan mold
3. Spritz with rubbing alcohol to get rid of bubbles
4. Let cool for 15 minutes

5. Cut soap with number cutters into the chosen year
6. Melt four oz of clear soap base in the microwave
7. Mix in 1 ml of champagne fragrance oil
8. Add two scoops of heavy metal gold mica
9. Pour a *thin* ⅛ inch layer into one rectangle mold and spray with rubbing alcohol
10. Let cool for five minutes, frequently stir to avoid a skin forming
11. Pour another thin layer on top and add your numbers
12. The numbers should be placed *backwards*
13. For an optional step, paint the year before onto the outside so it will be "washed away" and the new year will be revealed

13

BIRTHDAY CAKE SOAP WITH FROSTING
HOLIDAY RECIPE

Ingredients:

- 46 oz white melt
- 12 ml Hungarian lavender essential oil
- 5 ml buttercream & snickerdoodle fragrance oil
- 7 ml creamsicle cybilla fragrance oil
- Ultramarine violet color block
- Tangerine wow color block
- 5 ml vanilla color stabilizer
- 10" silicone loaf mold

Frosting Ingredients:

- 8 oz white melt
- 2 oz liquid castile soap base
- 3 ml buttercream and snickerdoodle fragrance oil
- 3 ml Vanilla color stabilizer

Directions:

1. Cut 12 oz of white melt and melt in a heat safe container
2. Heat soap for 30 second intervals, stir each time
3. Shave off of Ultraviolet color block and add until you reach your desired color
4. Add 4 ml of Lavender essential oil and stir
5. Pour lavender soap into loaf mold and spray with rubbing alcohol to rid of bubbles
6. Use the end of a paintbrush to draw deep grooves into the slightly hardened lavender soap

7. Set the mold aside and begin to make second layer
8. Cut and melt 8 oz of white melt and add 5 ml of buttercream and snickerdoodle fragrance oil.
9. Add 5 ml of vanilla color stabilizer to keep the soap white
10. Add layers together as quickly as possible
11. Use the same technique to create grooves as soon as the white mix has solidified yet not hardened completely
12. Melt 12 oz of cubed white melt in a heat safe container.
13. Heat at 30 second intervals, stirring between bursts
14. Shave off thin slices of Tangerine color block and stir into mixture until you have reached the desired color
15. Stir in 7 ml of creamsicle fragrance
16. Spray the white layer with rubbing alcohol and pour in the orange layer using the same technique of creating grooves as the two times before
17. Cut and melt 14 oz of white melt and pour into a heat safe container
18. Heat the soap on 30 second bursts, stirring every time in between.
19. Shave off chunks of Ultramarine violet color block into the mixture
20. Add 8 ml of lavender essential oil and stir until all things are combined
21. Spray orange soap layer with rubbing alcohol and pour on top of orange layer

Directions for Frosting:

1. Melt 8 oz of white melt into large container and add two oz of liquid castile soap base
2. Add 3 ml of vanilla color stabilizer and 3 ml of buttercream fragrance oil together
3. Use a hand mixer to whip the mixture together.
4. Begin on medium and turn to high after one minute
5. Mix until the frosting peaks
6. Use a spatula to quickly frost the top of the solidified soap
7. Once the soap is fully hardened, slice into rectangles

14

AMERICAN FLAG - PRESIDENTS DAY BAR SOAP

HOLIDAY RECIPE

Ingredients:

- White melt
- Clear melt
- Non - bleeding red liquid color
- Non - bleeding blue liquid color
- Iridescent Glitter

Directions:

1. Add 1 heaping tsp to 8 oz of clear, melted soap
2. Keep stirring until the glitter suspends in the soap
3. Soap will be thick and soupy before it will evenly suspend
4. Pour into mold that is large enough for the soap to cover the entire span
5. Melt more clear soap with a non - bleeding red.
6. To get a true red, use a clear soap and not a white one.
7. In a separate mold, pour in the red soap
8. Depending on how hot you cooked the soap, it should take 5 to 15 minutes to create a hardened, thick skin
9. While you're waiting, cut the glitter soap into long strips
10. Spritz rubbing alcohol onto the first layer, the red, and then pour in the white, melted soap.
11. Wait for the white soap to cool but not harden
12. Submerge the clear glitter soap into the white

13. Wait for this layer to harden with a thick skin, enough to hold another layer of soap.
14. Prepare the blue soap
15. Pour the blue soap onto the other layers and wait for all three layers to harden completely.
16. Cut the soap into rectangles and enjoy your patriotic soap

VALENTINE'S DAY SOAP

HOLIDAY RECIPE

Ingredients:

- Clear soap base
- Microwavable container
- Essential / fragrance oil
- Color block of your choice
- Silicone heart shaped mold

Directions:

1. Chop up roughly the amount you'll need for your silicone heart shaped mold
2. Melt the soap in the microwavable container at thirty second increments
3. Add in your coloring and your desired amount of fragrance - essential oils

4. Pour your soap into your molds
5. Let your soaps sit until they are fully hardened

16

NATIONAL WOMEN'S DAY

(FEMININE WASH)

Ingredients:

- ½ cup alcohol free witch hazel
- ½ cup rose water
- 1 tsp unscented castile soap
- 3 tsp almond oil or fractionated coconut oil
- 6 drops of lavender essential oil
- 1 foaming soap pump

Directions:

1. You can either add all ingredients straight to the bottle and swish it to stir, or you can mix them in a glass measuring cup and pour into the bottle.

LUCKY SHAMROCK SOAPS

ST. PATRICKS DAY SOAP

Ingredients:

- 2 pounds, 8 oz clear melt
- 8 oz white melt
- Shamrock mold
- Loaf mold
- Opalescent green mica
- Iridescent glitter
- Emerald green
- Non - bleeding oxide green
- Green tea fragrance or essential oil
- Rubbing alcohol

Directions:

1. Use the emerald green and non - bleeding green

oxide, clear melt, and green tea fragrance to make the shamrocks
2. Let shamrocks to sit over night
3. Take 8 oz of clear soap and melt in the microwave with 30 second bursts
4. Stir until it is no longer steaming and there are absolutely no chunks
5. Fragrance this soap with .1 to .2 oz of fragrance oil
6. Pour this soap into the loaf mold and spritz with rubbing alcohol
7. Spritz the shamrocks with rubbing alcohol as well and embed them into the soap that is already in the loaf mold (should fit about three shamrocks)
8. Allow a thick skin to form
9. Pour a layer of white soap over the top of the shamrocks
10. Allow to harden
11. Pour a thin layer of clear soap colored with the iridescent mica
12. Spray with rubbing alcohol to rid of any bubbles
13. Let sit overnight then carefully cut into three squares to show the shamrocks

EASTER EGG SOAPS

HOLIDAY RECIPE

Ingredients:

- ½ tsp yellow mica
- .4 oz passion fruit fragrance oil
- 3 oz clear soap base
- 16 oz white soap base
- 1 Easter egg mold
- Iridescent glitter
- Syringe

Directions:

1. Melt two or three oz of white soap in the microwave at thirty second increments
2. Use the syringe to fill the creases and designs in the bottom of the egg mold
3. Let the soap fully cool and harden

4. Scrape off any excess soap
5. After filling the crevices
6. Melt two or three oz of clear soap and let it cool to 125 degrees
7. Pour a thin layer of this into the eggs and sprinkle with the glitter quickly so they set
8. Melt 13 or 14 oz of white soap in a microwavable container for thirty seconds at a time
9. Add and stir in 12 ml of the fragrance oil and your color for a nice pastel egg
10. When the soap has cooled a little bit, about 125 degrees, spritz the glitter layer with rubbing alcohol and pour in your new layer
11. Let the soap cool for about 6 hours and now they're ready for Easter!

EARTH DAY SOAPS

HOLIDAY SOAPS

Ingredients:

- 9 oz olive oil
- 9 oz coconut oil
- 9 oz palm oil
- 3 oz castor oil
- 2 oz mango butter
- 4.5 oz lye
- 10.5 oz distilled water
- 4 tsp rhassoul clay
- 1 oz essential oil (optional)

Directions:

1. Prepare your protective wear
2. Pour 10.5 oz of distilled water into a jar

3. Slowly pour 4.5 oz of lye into the water until it is completely dissolved
4. Let the lye mixture cool until it has reached 100 degrees.
5. As the lye cools, mix all other ingredients except the essential oils in your slow - cooker
6. Once they are all melted, remove the oils from the heat and add the clay. Use a stick blender to mix the clay until it is completely gone.
7. Let oils cool until they have reached 100 degrees
8. When the temperatures of the oils and lye match, slowly add the lye to the oils and use your stick blender to mix until trace
9. Now add your essential oils
10. Pour the batter into your soap molds, still wearing your protective gear
11. Place the mold somewhere it won't be disturbed for 24 hours and cover with an upside-down cardboard box
12. Let the soap sit for 24 hours and then let them stand in a dry area for 4 to 6 weeks

CINCO DE MAYO SOAPS

Ingredients:

- 5.5 oz avocado oil
- 8.3 oz canola oil
- 13.8 oz coconut oil
- 13.8 oz olive oil
- 13.8 oz palm oil
- 7.7 oz sodium hydroxide lye
- 18.2 distilled water
- Titanium dioxide
- Merlot sparkle mica
- Electric bubble gum colorant
- Green chrome oxide pigment
- 1.4 oz lime fragrance oil
- 1.6 oz bay leaf fragrance oil
- 5-pound mold with sliding bottom
- Silicone liner for 5 lb wood mold
- Multi - pour sectioning tool

Directions:

1. Wear gloves and long sleeves
2. Slowly add the lye to water and stir gently until all the lye has dissolved and the liquid is clear
3. Melt and mix the coconut oil, avocado oil, canola oil, palm oil, and olive oils
4. Once both the lye and the oils cool to 130 or slightly below, add the lye water to the oils and stick blend
5. Add 1 tsp of sodium lactate to the mix
6. As the batter reaches a thin trace, separate it all into three equal containers
7. In the first container put in all the titanium dioxide
8. In the second container add 2 tsp. Of merlot sparkle mica and 1 tsp electric bubble gum colorant
9. In the third container mix in 1 tsp green chrome oxide
10. Add the specific fragrance oils to each container and whisk thoroughly
11. Stir more with the stick blender if the concoction seems too thin
12. Pour the various colors into the three sections of the mold, make sure each have an equal amount of soap in them
13. Be sure not to overfill so the colors don't mix
14. Once all sections have been equally filled, remove the center piece and set aside
15. Once the soaps have slightly hardened, remove the two dividers straight up and set aside as well

16. Inset a chopstick or dowel into the very top of the soap that is between two of the color stripes
17. Make small S's along the color divide to gently mix the two shades of soap
18. Spritz the top of the soap with rubbing alcohol to rid of any bubbles
19. Let the soap set in the mold for 3 to 4 days before removing it
20. Once the mold is hardened, cut them into rectangles
21. Let the bars cure for 4 to 6 weeks before use

MOTHER'S DAY SOAP

HOLIDAY SOAP

Ingredients:

- 300 gram coconut oil
- 250 gram olive oil
- 250 gram rice bran oil
- 150 gram palm oil
- 50 gram shea butter
- 142 gram sodium hydroxide
- 270 gram filtered water (plus ¼ aloe Vera juice - add to oils)
- 20 ml blackberry fragrance oil
- Pink and blue ultramarine oxides dispersed in liquid glycerin; titanium dioxide powder ½ tsp.

Directions:

1. Make lye mixture and let cool to 30 degrees

2. Add titanium dioxide powder to oils or aloe juice depending on whether it is liquid or oil dispersible.
3. Bring oils to 30 degrees
4. Add aloe vera juice to oils before the lye solution
5. Add 15 drops of pink and 5 drops of blue coloration
6. Add in fragrance
7. Let harden completely

FATHER'S DAY COFFEE SOAP

COFFEE SCENTED SOAP

Ingredients:

- 6 oz hot purified water
- 1 tsp coffee grounds
- 2 oz lye
- 5 oz coconut oil
- 5 oz olive oil
- 6 oz soybean oil (also known as vegetable oil)

Directions:

1. Mix coffee in with hot water and allow to cool
2. Mix the lye and coffee water together until the lye is completely dissolved
3. Allow to cool again between 120 to 130 degrees
4. Combine all oils and heat to about 120 degrees as well

5. Once all ingredients are close in temperature, mix the oils and coffee solution together
6. Stir with a stick blender for about 5 - 6 minutes
7. Pour into your mold and cover
8. Set aside your soap for a few days, allowing it to harden
9. Cut and let air for three weeks before use

SPOOKY HALLOWEEN SOAP
HOLIDAY SOAP

Ingredients:

- 12 bar square silicone mold
- 32 oz Stephenson jelly melt and pour base
- .3 oz Apple jack peel fragrance oil
- .3 oz spellbound woods cybilla fragrance oil
- .3 oz vanilla color stabilizer
- 2 ml green apple coloring
- 2 ml Easter purple coloring
- Small spider toys

Directions:

1. Cut the jelly melt into small pieces
2. Put in a large, heat safe container
3. Melt at 1 minute intervals
4. Stir between each one

5. Split soap into two even containers
6. In one container add one fragrance and vanilla color stabilizer
7. Do the same to the other container but with the other fragrance
8. Stir gently
9. Add the green dye to the container with the apple jack fragrance oil and the purple to the other container and gently stir
10. If the soap begins to harden, put back into the microwave in thirty second bursts
11. Put the spider toys into the molds and slowly pour the two different colored soaps into different molds
12. Allow to harden for 4 hours then remove from the mold
13. Wrap soap in plastic wrap

THANKSGIVING SOAP RECIPE

Ingredients:

- Jelly roll pan
- Festive seasonal cookie cutter
- Clear melt
- Soap syringe injector
- Micas in fall colors
- Spray bottle of rubbing alcohol
- Pumpkin spice fragrance oil

Directions:

1. Prepare soap for cookie cutter portion. Try coloring with a brown
2. Pour the soap into the jelly roll pan - it holds about 8 oz
3. Spritz with rubbing alcohol and allow to harden

4. Gently remove the soap from the mold and use your cookie cutter to create holiday shapes
5. Prepare clear soap, microwaving it at 30 second intervals
6. Once the soap is melted, add fragrance
7. Pour soap into three small pots. You want .5 oz to 1 oz of soap per pot
8. Colorize each a vibrant fall color
9. Pour a thin layer of clear soap into the jelly roll pan and wait for the soap to harden
10. Spray the clear soap with rubbing alcohol and your cut-out shape
11. Place the shape onto the clear soap
12. Take your syringe and fill it with your colorized soap
13. Spray the clear soap and cut out with alcohol and use your syringe to draw squiggles on top - do as many as you'd like
14. Prepare your background soap as any color you'd like the same as you prepared your other soaps
15. Spritz your hardened soap with alcohol and pour in your freshly made soap
16. Let the soap fully harden for a few hours before peeling it out of the mold
17. Cut it into squares and wrap the soap in saran wrap

CHRISTMAS SOAP

HOLIDAY SOAP

Ingredients:

- Gingerbread man mold
- 12.5 oz goat milk melt
- 7.5 oz clear melt
- Fizzy lemonade colorant
- Neon blue raspberry colorant
- Liquid yellow
- Liquid blue
- Liquid red oxide
- Liquid non - bleeding cherry
- Liquid black iron oxide
- Liquid non - bleeding teal
- Liquid green oxide
- Liquid glycerin
- .15 cc mini scoop
- 5 ml almond cybilla fragrance oil
- 5 ml cinnamon sugar fragrance oil

- 10 ml vanilla color stabilizer
- Box template for gingerbread man

Directions:

1. In a small bowl, add ten .15 cc mini scoops of fizzy lemonade color and ½ tsp liquid glycerin.
2. Use a mini mixer to remove all chunks
3. In a separate bowl, dispense four .15 cc mini scoops of neon blue raspberry into 1 tsp of 99% rubbing alcohol
4. Use a mini mixer to remove all chunks
5. Set both colors aside
6. In a large microwavable bowl, cut and melt 12.5 oz goat milk melt in the microwave using 15 second bursts
7. Stir between each
8. Add 2 ml almond fragrance oil to the clear melt along with 2 ml cinnamon sugar fragrance oil and 4 ml vanilla color stabilizer
9. Gently stir
10. Add 3 ml almond fragrance oil, 3 ml cinnamon sugar fragrance oil and 6 ml vanilla color stabilizer to the goat milk melt
11. Thoroughly combine by gently stirring
12. Gather four heat safe containers
13. In the first container add 5 oz of goat milk melt
14. In the second container add another 5 oz of goat milk melt
15. In the third container add 2 oz goat milk melt and 3 oz clear melt

16. In the fourth container add .5 oz goat milk melt and 4.5 oz clear melt
17. In the first container add half of the neon blue raspberry and one drop of liquid blue
18. Stir thoroughly
19. To the second container add 10 mini scoops of fizzy lemonade and the rest of the neon blue raspberry and 3 drops of liquid yellow
20. Stir thoroughly
21. To the third container add 2 drops of non - bleeding teal liquid, 5 drops of liquid green, 2 drops of liquid black and 2 drops of liquid blue
22. Stir thoroughly
23. To the fourth container add 6 drops of liquid red, 2 drops of non - bleeding cherry liquid, 2 drops of liquid yellow and one drop of liquid black
24. Stir thoroughly
25. To fill in the small details on the gingerbread man, use the syringe tool.
26. Remember to fill in the lines around the edges as well as the face and bow
27. Clean up any messes
28. Allow the designs to fully harden and cool down
29. Re-melt the soaps in the four containers
30. Pour the soaps into the gingerbread man molds and spritz with rubbing alcohol
31. Allow the soaps to fully harden

26

I HOPE YOU ENJOYED MY CREATIONS

REMEMBER TO BE SAFE WHEN WORKING WITH ALL MATERIALS!

I hope you enjoy these recipes and put them to good use. You can also feel free to experiment with different colors and textures and make your own creations! Experiment with various molds and see what you are capable of creating!

www.ingramcontent.com/pod-product-compliance
Lightning Source LLC
Chambersburg PA
CBHW020548080526
44583CB00013B/1056